Abraham Lincoln
A LIFE OF RESPECT

by Sheila Rivera

Lerner Publications Company • Minneapolis

Photo Acknowledgments

The images in this book are reproduced with permission of: © Todd Strand/Independent Picture Service, p. 4; Photographs and Prints Division, Schomburg Center for Research in Black Culture, The New York Public Library, Astor, Lenox and Tilden Foundations, p. 6; Library of Congress, pp. 8 (LC-USZ62-2582), 10 (LC-USZ61-2172), 11 (LC-USZ62-4377), 12 (LC-USZC4-2472), 16 (LC-USZ62-35077), 20 (LC-USZC4-1796), 23 (LC-USZ62-1287), 24 (LC-USZ62-175); © Kean Collection/Hulton Archives, Getty Images, p. 9; Illinois State Historical Library, p. 13; © The Lincoln Museum, Fort Wayne Indiana, p. 14; © Bettmann/CORBIS, p. 18; © West Virginia Archives, p. 19; © North Wind Picture Archives, p. 22; © SuperStock, p. 26; Minneapolis Public Library Informational Center, p. 27. Front Cover: © CORBIS.

Text copyright © 2006 by Lerner Publications Company

Lerner Publications Company
A division of Lerner Publishing Group
241 First Avenue North
Minneapolis, MN 55401 U.S.A.

Website address: www.lernerbooks.com

Words in **bold type** are explained in a glossary on page 31.

Library of Congress Cataloging-in-Publication Data

Rivera, Sheila, 1970–
    Abraham Lincoln : a life of respect / by Sheila Rivera.
      p.   cm. – (Pull ahead books)
    Includes index.
    ISBN-13: 978–0–8225–3473–0 (lib. bdg. : alk. paper)
    ISBN-10: 0–8225–3473–8 (lib. bdg. : alk. paper)
    1. Lincoln, Abraham, 1809–1865–Juvenile literature. 2. Presidents–United States–Biography–Juvenile literature. I. Title. II. Series.
E457.905.R58 2006
973.7'092–dc22   2005009040

Manufactured in the United States of America
1 2 3 4 5 6 – JR – 11 10 09 08 07 06

Table of Contents

4

Who Is Abraham Lincoln?

Do you know whose face appears on the penny? It is Abraham Lincoln's! He was the sixteenth president of the United States. Abraham was a **respectful** person. He was kind and fair to everyone he met.

These people were forced to work in a cotton field.

Slavery Is Wrong

Abraham was born in 1809. During the 1800s, many black people in the United States were **slaves.** Slaves had to do whatever their white owners told them to do. They were not allowed to make choices for themselves.

Owners sold slaves.

When he was a young man, Abraham saw slaves being sold.

Abraham did not think it was right for one person to own another person.

Slave owners watch slaves as they work.

Thomas Lincoln, Abraham's father

Abraham's father felt that slavery was wrong.

Abraham also felt that slavery was wrong. Like his father, Abraham respected others.

Abraham Lincoln

When Abraham grew up, he did a variety of jobs. He worked in a post office. He also measured land.

Abraham worked hard at everything he did.

Abraham owned this store.

Abraham bought a store. He did not
sell enough **goods,** so Abraham had
to close the store.

Abraham studied hard.

Abraham was interested in government. He studied law and became a **lawyer.**

Abraham also gave speeches. He told people that slavery was not right.

Abraham enjoyed giving speeches.

Abraham became president.

President Lincoln

In 1861, Abraham was **elected** president of the United States. At that time, people who lived in the South still allowed slavery in their states. People who lived in the North did not. Abraham wanted to stop slavery from spreading to more states.

Slaves did most of the fieldwork for whites in the South.

People who owned slaves were angry. They thought that Abraham would take away their slaves.

People in the South decided they did not want to be part of the United States anymore.

The South began to fight.

The Civil War began.

Civil War

A war began between the North and the South. It was called the Civil War. Abraham did not want people to fight. He wanted to keep the country together. He was very worried.

Abraham continued to talk about slavery. He said that all people deserved respect. He believed that everyone should be free.

In 1862, Abraham said that slaves in the South were free.

Slaves were thankful for their freedom.

Slaves celebrated.

Free at Last!

An **amendment** was added to the **Constitution.** The Constitution lists the rights that all Americans have. The amendment said that no person could own another person. Abraham agreed with this new amendment.

Everyone was glad that the war ended.

In 1865, the Civil War ended. Many
people died during the war. But the
country was united once more.

Abraham respected the people who had fought in the war. And he was glad that the country was whole again.

President Lincoln respected his country and its people.

ABRAHAM LINCOLN TIMELINE

1809
Abraham Lincoln is born on February 12.

1861
The Civil War begins.

1861
Abraham becomes president of the United States.

1862
Abraham says that no one in the South can own slaves after January 1, 1863.

1865

The Thirteenth Amendment to the Constitution makes slavery illegal.

1865

Abraham dies on April 15.

1865

The Civil War ends.

More about Abraham Lincoln

- Abraham was considered a great speaker. One of his most famous speeches was the Gettysburg Address.

- Abraham's picture is on both the penny and the five-dollar bill.

- Abraham only went to school for about one year.

Websites

Biography of Abraham Lincoln
http://www.whitehouse.gov/history/presidents/al16.html

The History Place Presents Abraham Lincoln
http://www.historyplace.com/lincoln/

U.S. Presidents–Abraham Lincoln
http://www.whitehouse.gov/kids/presidents/
abrahamlincoln.html

Glossary

amendment: a change made to correct, add something, or make something better

Constitution: a document that lists the rights guaranteed to all Americans. It also explains the job of the government.

elected: chosen by voting

goods: things that can be bought and sold

lawyer: a person who is trained to help others understand laws and help them in court

respectful: treating someone with honor and care

slaves: people who are owned by other people

Index